Ready To Rise

62 Ways You and Your Business Can Thrive & Grow in Challenging Times

Curated by Helen Vandenberghe

Lead Editor and Curator, Helen Vandenberghe

www.readytorise.co.uk

Limits of Liability and Disclaimer of Warranty

Warning – Disclaimer

Welcome to Ready to Rise

This book is about hope, courage, and wisdom. It began as a spark of an idea, just a few short weeks before publication, a testament to how rapidly things can change, and how brilliantly people can pull together. Here's how it began.

In early Spring 2020, here in the UK, we were reeling from the shock of an imminent pandemic.

Many people in my community of entrepreneurs and business owners were experiencing fear, uncertainty, and despair as they saw their day-to-day routines, along with their livelihoods disappear in front of their eyes.

Suddenly we were all worried about our elderly relatives, home-educating the children, and wondering if the supermarkets would have the basic necessities we'd previously taken for granted. Not to mention the shocking daily news of thousands of people 'just like us', contracting the disease.

For those of us who were self-employed or running a business, the challenge became figuring out how to 'pivot' and turn our enterprises into something we could run from home. Or for many, sadly, facing the prospect of closing down, or putting their business 'on hold'.

We have never seen such massive change to the global and local business landscape in such a short period of time.

However, amidst all this anxiety and concern, **I started to receive messages of encouragement and hope**. By email, in WhatsApp groups, on social media, there were voices of resilience. Some focused on acceptance, some on health, and some on forging new ways forward for your business.

I wanted a place to collect all these kind words of encouragement, tips, and wisdom, and to share them with the wider world... and so the 'Ready to Rise' book project began.

I put a call out for contributors and was amazed, as people from across the world sat down and wrote heartfelt stories and words of advice. Within 21 days, the entire book was created, and getting ready to be published.

In this book you'll find tips on pivoting your marketing, staying grounded, and keeping well, along with words of encouragement to lift you up on tough days.

Our contributors include Septuagenarian entrepreneurs, TV personalities, best-selling authors, and first-time writers. You'll hear from people from Asia, Africa, North America, Australia, and Europe.

Whatever you're facing right now, and wherever you are in the world, we hope this book provides comfort, guidance, and support.

Helen Vandenbeghe

Business & Book Mentor, Author, & International Speaker. Helping coaches and entrepreneurs become successful, published authors, in-demand speakers, and high-end course creators.

www.ReadytoRise.co.uk
http://www.getclientsfast.net/

www.WriteYourBook.Biz

P.S. *We decided to keep most of the writing in the author's home language, with as little editing as possible. so you may find a mixture of UK & American English, and we appreciate your flexibility and understanding.*

This helped us get this book out extremely quickly - without massive re-writing. We're all learning to adapt right now & I strongly believe done is better than perfect:)

About Helen Vandenberghe

Known as the 'mentor to rising stars', Helen Vandenberghe helps coaches and entrepreneurs become successful, published authors, in-demand speakers, and high-end course creators.

An international coach, author, and speaker, she works with new and seasoned coaches and business owners to turn their passion into profit and establish them as thought-leaders in their field.

After breaking free from a corporate role as CEO of an International Training Company, Helen has built three successful companies - and had a fair few 'life lessons' along the way.

Helen has trained over a thousand business leaders, and is the founder of Get Published Fast and Get Clients Fast. Discover more at

www.GetClientsFast.net,
www.writeyourbook.biz
www.readytorise.co.uk

Free Tools and Resources
For You!

It has been wonderful to see so many organisations and individuals creating wonderful resources to help us all as we cope with the changes we are experiencing.

From online concerts, to business advice, virtual classes in everything from yoga to drawing, the world is demonstrating just how generous we can be.

As these change all the time, we've put together our favourite resources online.

Access your gifts and join our wonderful community at:

www.ReadyToRiseGifts.Online

Getting The Most Out of

Ready To Rise

This book is designed to help you thrive and grow, as you face your own unique challenges during and following the recent global health crisis.

With over two month's worth of daily inspiration, we hope you'll 'dip in to' it each day reflecting on that day's entry.

Maybe you could start a journal and write your thoughts and any actions you've taken?

We'd love to hear how the book has helped you and any particular 'aha' moments you've had.

Why not connect with us at our Facebook Group **HERE**, and share your stories **(https://bit.ly/2SKsPTm).**
You never know, you might be featured in our next book!

Also, PLEASE write us a review at **Amazon.co.uk** -this makes a huge difference to our authors and also helps us reach even more people.

Table Of Contents

Attitude of Opportunity

Attitude of Opportunity

Mary Silver MSW

"Challenges are the Universe's way of saying "Get Creative!"

In times of difficulty there is one fool-proof way that you can stay on track, manifest your desires, and attract the very best that the situation has to offer. You may not be able to change the circumstances of the situation, but you can change your experience of the circumstances.

The best way you can change the outcome during difficult times and ensure that you come out in the best position possible is to change your attitude about what you're going through. Your attitude will dictate what experience you attract into your life.

Say you want to grow your business but everything in your reality is saying that's not likely. If your attitude stays in the vibration of lack, meaning you believe you can't grow your business, then you will have a hard time attracting clients to you.

When you have a positive attitude and believe you can grow your business during difficult times you allow yourself to see opportunities that will help you grow. You see the problem differently which opens your mind to new possibilities.

Direct your attitude towards prosperity and watch how your opportunities show up! Do this for 30 days and begin to experience your desires!

Mary Silver MSW is a business and success coach helping service providers become profitable by mastering their sales process. You can find out more about her by visiting **www.marybaileysilver.com**

Tips for Self(care) Isolation

Tips for Self(care) Isolation

Janey Lee Grace

'Self-care is really about taking care of you and focusing on feeling good about yourself - mind and body'
Franchesca Ramsey

We can't control much, but we can control our thoughts and focus on boosting our immunity and mindset.

S- Sobriety. There has never been a better time to be sober, Cut down or ditch the booze, you'll have more energy and sleep better. Alcohol lowers immunity and increases anxiety.

E- Exercise. Take online classes, Pilates, Yoga and workouts, walk in nature!

L – Love. Self-love is critical, be kind to yourself and others. Practice your community spirit. Love in action.

F- Focus. What do you want for yourself? How can you improve your skills and adapt your business?

C- Connection. Find your tribe and do something creative. Encourage each other to learn a language, get baking, singing, painting, knitting, gardening ….all the 'ING's'.

A- Appreciation. Keep gratitude lists and stay encouraged, uplifted and inspired.

R-Resources. What tops up your battery levels? Walking,

dance, art, reading? You also need practical resources such as good nutrition and supplements to boost immunity.

E- Energy. Stay grounded, take off your shoes and stand or lie on the earth, Practice meditation and visualization.

Stay well and Positive!

Janey Lee Grace is a presenter, author of 5 wellbeing books and runs The Sober Club, an online community for people wanting to live their best life without the booze
www.thesoberclub.com

The Marie Kondo Self-Care Hack

The Marie Kondo Self-Care Hack

Jenn Summers

"Those who love you most help you to love yourself."

There are times in our lives when we need to clean up, declutter, and do what is best for us. Sometimes that means the relationships in our lives too.

Unfortunately, many times we leave self-care until something drastic has happened and we are forced to do it. That's ok, there is no better time than now.

Where does Marie Kondo come into all of this? Well, if you have watched her show or read her book you will know that she asks you to evaluate whether an item brings you joy.

So in turn, does this relationship bring you joy? Does it make you go 'oooh'?

Have you outgrown them? Do they now bring you a negative experience? Maybe it is time to let them go.

If so, then package the relationship up nice and neat and send it on its way. Or use this time of distancing to do just that, distance yourself.

You are the most important person in your life and the relationships in your life alter your self-identity. Surround yourself with people who love you unconditionally- even if right now that's just virtually or on the phone. When your life is filled with love then you can find the core elements of your own wellbeing.

Jenn Summers is a Goal Strategist Life Coach. Her passion is helping people to love themselves so that they can achieve greatness. Grab her free eBook on toxic relationships here:

https://bit.ly/2WdCc03

See an Opportunity to

make real connections again

See an Opportunity to make real connections again

Claire Carroll

"In a world of crisis some will thrive while others survive. Don't be the opportunistic, however absolutely see the opportunity! And know the difference ..."

In time of crisis maybe you need to pull away from automation in your business and go back to authentic connections.

Reach out like a real person, make connections, and collaborate, discuss how you can help one another.

Automation can work wonders and systems are great. However people need people and want to be heard.

Warmth & connection, 'old school' ways of networking. There's nothing more powerful than reaching out.

Create a group, connect, and understand their problems, share your solution to that problem.

Link arms and collaborate, help more numbers by linking arms with others that can also provide.

Create joint ventures so you are providing solutions in abundance, people are receiving large amounts of value and solutions from multiple sources.

Never be the opportunistic person! (Definition - Exploiting immediate opportunities, taking advantage of a crisis of those in need).

But do see the opportunity! (Definition - A time or set of circumstances that makes it possible to do something new).

Always Think outside the box!

There will always be people who survive & others that will thrive in a crisis….

Always come from the heart.

Please be the one to see an opportunity – don't be the opportunist!

Know the difference

Claire Carroll is an Online Business & Mindset Coach – For Women that know life begins at 40! Helping mature women to choose their niche & move forward online.

https://www.clairecarrollcoaching.com/

Time to Trust your Gut

Time to Trust your Gut

Jo Cowlin

"Listen to your intuition, it will tell you everything you need to know."

When faced with a crisis or called to perform under pressure you can easily find yourself in a cycle of overthinking. In a world where intellect is rewarded, many ignore the gut or use their intuition. Intuition is automatic, fast and occurs subconsciously whereas analytical thinking is slow, logical and conscious. Recognising and listening to your gut is important not only for business but for your mental health as well.

Why is it important?

- Trusting your gut is the ultimate act of trusting yourself.
- It helps you to avoid unhealthy situations and relationships.
- It is shaped by your past experiences and knowledge.

Here's how to practice:

1. Slow down and find stillness. This helps to recognise and process the information you are receiving.
2. Breathe slowly, notice and listen to the bodily sensations (changes in heart rate, breathing, muscle tension etc)
3. Be curious about what they are telling you.

4. Focus on what feels good. Tell yourself out loud what decision you are making and see how your body reacts to it. Or write it on a piece of paper, step into its energy field and notice the somatic response.

Use it or you lose it!

Jo Cowlin is an intuitive coach and facilitator who works with leaders and their teams to help them regroup, refocus and create exceptional results and can be found at:

www.jocowlin.com

Master Your Messaging

Master Your Messaging

Helen Vandenberghe

"We are stronger when we listen, and smarter when we share."- Rania Al-Abdullah

The world has changed irrevocably in just a few short months. It is vital that your communication keeps pace and adapts to the world we live in now. You may have automated emails, social media posts or pre-booked advertising that was perfectly appropriate when you wrote it, but now may not quite hit the right tone, or could even seem insensitive.

Tweak for relevance. Make sure your messaging reflects life as it is now, so check you don't have regular posts saying things like 'What's your favourite restaurant right now?' or 'Who crushed speaking gigs this week?'.

Create Comfort. Where relevant use phrases to reinforce the safety of your audience, such as 'virtual', 'in-home', 'contact-free' and 'online'.

Check for insensitive words and phrases such as 'killer deals', 'create contagious content', 'let's go viral'. With social media views at a peak, one small mistake could cost you dearly.

Shift and stay relevant. As the situation changes, adapt your messaging to the 'new normal'. What's going on for your customers now?

Stay optimistic - but don't over promise. Tell them what you do know - a positive but straight-talking approach is much more likely to be well received than 'internet marketing hype'.

It is perfectly legitimate to market to your audience during a crisis - but make sure you step into their shoes and really reflect life as it is now.

Helen Vandenberghe is known as the mentor to rising stars. She helps coaches and entrepreneurs become successful, published authors, in-demand speakers and high-end course creators. Discover how to reinvent your business at: **www.GetClientsFast.net**

Challenges are Opportunities To Grow or Merely Survive

Challenges are Opportunities To Grow or Merely Survive

Dorothy Martin-Neville

"You and your life – although completely unlimited - are exactly what you perceive them to be. What are you choosing to see?"

Whether we are speaking of a pandemic, bankruptcy, job loss, or even divorce, we can see any challenge we are confronted with as a crisis or simply as a challenge that is causing us to grow in ways we never would have consciously chosen.

A key question is, is the person who existed when this experience began going to be the same person who comes out the other end? That is totally a personal choice. If you have a business, is your business going to "survive" this challenge or is it going to come out as a greater reflection of the person you have become?

In any tough situation, it is imperative to build in time daily to stop and catch up with yourself. How are you getting through? Survival? Victim? Reacting? Responding? Honestly, you have the ability to move into any or all of these if you choose. Visit those states, don't stay there!

While we certainly need to deal with the day-to-day issues that develop, to keep it in perspective we also need to look at every situation from the 30,000-foot view. What change is calling you?

Dr. Dorothy Martin-Neville, founder or 4 companies, and author of 8 books, supports leaders in recognizing their visionary and leadership styles as they transition into new paradigms of success.

askdrdorothy.com

Staying Visible in a Crisis

Staying Visible in a Crisis

Julie Brown

*"Publicity can be terrible. But only if you don't have any." –
Jane Russell*

The world we operate in is changing fast but one thing that never changes is the importance of our business being visible. Our digital platforms and social media allows us to speak regularly to customers and respond to change quickly. This lets us continue to promote our business, even in a crisis and have an engaged audience ready to buy our services once it's over. Don't hide away.

Media coverage is a marketing tool like no other, putting our expertise in-front of an audience, helping attract new clients for free. It gives us credibility and marks us out as an expert in our field. These days that media might be a publication, TV programme, podcaster, YouTube channel, an Instagram influencer or a website.

If you're new to this, search for #journorequest on Twitter. Here you'll find a host of editors, journalists, bloggers, podcasters and TV researchers looking for business owners like you to contribute to their content. It's a fast-moving hashtag so look twice a day. If you see anything you'd like to get involved with, reply to the tweet or DM them and they'll do the rest. It's the easiest route into the powerhouse that is the media.

Julie Brown is a visibility and PR coach working with entrepreneurs on growing their audience. She is also a journalist of 17 years, most of those as editor-in-chief and publisher. Visit : **http://www.iamjuliebrown.com/**

Attitude Is Everything!

Attitude Is Everything!

Dr Kevin Lentin

"Now, more than ever, 'Your attitude, not your aptitude, will determine your altitude." – Zig Ziglar'

Attitude is a 'state of existence', almost a 'state of being', and the really good news is that it is DIRECTLY under your control.

The importance of your attitude on the way each and every one of your cells function cannot be underestimated. Attitude applies to everything and is what I call a 'Pro-Life' message. The 'quality' of that message is critical to optimum body function.

Managing life is, seriously, so much easier when your attitude is upbeat, positive, accepting, devoid of the need for conflict, separate from the good opinion of others and full of gratitude.

Affirmations are powerful 'attitude drivers'.

Repeating these, on your own, over and over, will 'drive' the 'half full' attitude into your subconscious:

I am in direct control of my attitude

I choose to have a positive attitude

I radiate an attitude of gratitude

I am gratitude personified

I love life and everything it has to offer

I am a positive being radiating love

I choose to vibrate at a positive, loving and serving level

I choose to see good in everything

Dr. Kevin Lentin is a chiropractor with a special interest in the promotion of structural, nutritional and psychological health through 1:1 consulting, public presentations and online coaching, training and mentoring.

www.drkevinlentin.life

Unlock Your Radiance And Make More Money & Impact

Unlock Your Radiance and Make More Money & Impact

Minling Chuang

"I reclaim my power. I reclaim my voice. I reclaim my inner radiance."

Your radiance attracts clients to you, not the logos or your website. Every brand has an energy vibration and frequency it emits and people can either feel connected or repelled as a result. Understanding your energy is key to people falling in love with your brand.

1. Release

Emotions, fears, and anxiety can be triggered during a crisis and until it's released, it will always be in the background.

To release, ask yourself, "What lesson do I get to learn from this emotion?" This question allows you to see new insights and make peace with the emotion.

2. Reclaim

Your voice is the most powerful tool you have. Reclaiming your voice inspires your audience to see you as a leader they want to follow.

Every morning, say the affirmation "I am confident & I fully own my voice" in front of a mirror and embody the feeling of being in your power.

3. Radiate

Radiance starts from the inside. You must feel good and love yourself before others love you.

Increase the fun and playfulness in your business. People are attracted to people who make them feel happy. When you're authentically having fun, it builds likeability and trust with your audience.

Minling Chuang helps her clients unleash their inner radiance to become the ONLY brand their clients love to buy. Leveraging 10+ years in branding to help her clients shine online.

http://brandfameschool.com

Be A Butterfly

Be A Butterfly

Dr. Trina Boice

"How does one become a butterfly? You must want to fly so much that you are willing to give up being a caterpillar."

A caterpillar is a cute, fuzzy, lovely little creature. There's nothing wrong with it, but it lives on the ground and has limited vision and ability. Once it morphs into a butterfly, it has wings that can take it higher and farther, living a more elevated life.

Do you feel that transformation happening in your own life now? This crazy pandemic has gifted us with a unique opportunity to put aside bad habits or get out of an unhealthy rut in our lives. Being stuck at home has given us a unique chance to look at how we spend our lives and decide what's truly important to us. Think of this quarantine as your time to be in your cocoon, transforming into something even better. Like a butterfly, we can emerge from this worldwide crisis either a frazzled, exhausted caterpillar or a rejuvenated butterfly with enlightened vision. We can't control what's happening in the world, but we can control the way we respond. Choose to be a butterfly.

Dr. Trina Boice teaches at BYU, is known as YouTuber "Movie Review Mom" and podcasts "Daily Inspirational Quote With Trina Boice." She's an author of 30 books and online courses at **www.LifelongLearningEducation.com**

Take Your Business Online

Take Your Business Online

Helen Vandenberghe

"The measure of intelligence is the ability to change." —
Albert Einstein

If you normally provide in-person services, you may need to 'pivot' online to stay solvent right now. You and your clients may be 'stuck at home' but that doesn't mean you can't serve them. Here's some ideas to reinvent your offering and generate revenue NOW!

Offer Sessions Online. Offer your usual services as an online session. Many personal trainers have been able to create innovative home work-outs and deliver them simply over zoom or skype.

Teach Something New. If your main business can't operate right now, do you have a complimentary skill you could offer? A local decorator is running an interior design service online. A massage therapist who happens to be an ex-teacher is fully booked helping parents plan their 'instant homeschooling schedule', along with virtual tutoring for kids. Get creative!

Create a Course. Pick a hot topic that your clients want to learn about and create an online course.

Deliver Your Goods! One nutritionist I know has started a 'smoothie delivery service', ideal for people who can't get out to the shops. An independent bookshop in New York has teamed up with a local food delivery company who will deliver books, stationery and gifts, along with your pizza!

Offer Gift Vouchers. If you really can't offer your services 'virtually', create packages for future services. In the UK a hairdresser and beauty therapist created an 'Post Lockdown Pamper Package' for when things get 'back to normal'. She gets paid now, the client has something to look forward to! Genius! You could sell these online through **eventbrite,** via **paypal** or even at **Etsy**, if you bundled it with a physical gift.

Get creative and get out there!

Helen Vandenberghe has been helping business owners get clients fast for over a decade. Join her FREE facebook group **The Client Attraction Club** for ideas and inspiration.(**https://bit.ly/2WasZp2**).

From
'Stuck' To 'Safe'

From 'Stuck' To 'Safe'

Irene Gannaway

"I don't think of all the misery, but of the beauty that still remains." – Anne Frank

At times like this, we can feel like we have lost so much. Our day-to-day lives have been turned upside down.

My daughter Wendy visited me today (from a safe distance!) dropping off prescriptions and other essentials I couldn't get online – it was hard not being able to just reach over and hug her, like 'normal'.

We talked briefly about Terry Waite – the British Humanitarian who was taken hostage for over four years in Beirut – much of it in solitary confinement. In a recent interview he recommended a change of mindset from being 'stuck' inside to being 'safe' at home.

It made me think of Anne Frank's ordeal. I am so grateful to be free to move around my home, play music, watch TV etc. without the constant fear Anne & her family endured.

Sometimes we just need to shift our perspective from sadness to gratitude.

Stay home, stay safe & stay grateful for what you still have.

Irene Gannaway is not just an inspirational Mum. Irene devoted 22 years to the Samaritans including 2 years as Director, where she undertook many keynote speaking engagements and press interviews.

How To Ethically Profit From Chaos

How To Ethically Profit From Chaos

Tom Matzen

"The time to profit is when there is blood in the streets, even if the blood is your own". ~ Nathan Rothschild

If you're an entrepreneur, small business owner or service professional that wants to not only survive the chaos and panic in the marketplace right now, but come out the other side thriving, now is the time to recognize this, and put a strategic plan in place. Three keys to success:

Recognize there are five ways to be paid: be utilized, be enhanced, be appreciated, be referred and be paid cash (thanks to direct marketing rock star Brian Kurtz);

Sell on value not price, so you can create Raving Fans;

They're more loyal when you mess up

They're willing spend to more with you

And, they refer people, unsolicited.

Build multiple referral programs now so you can accelerate your word of mouth marketing rapidly as the chaos lifts and we get to experience the "new norm". Conduct Show Them We Care calls, ask for Referrals, create sweepstakes, install Loyalty Apps and more. Now is the time to create at least five referral programs.

Your tribe needs you, your team needs you, your family and friends need you.

Time to step up and make it happen.

Tom Matzen has started 82 businesses, built seven to seven figures and beyond. His mission is to empower 10,000 Authority Entrepreneurs to build 7 & 8 figure businesses by 2025. Discover more Here:

https://bit.ly/2WcOXYP

Health Is Wealth, Especially Right Now

Health Is Wealth, Especially Right Now

Irina Strunina

"People sacrifice their health in order to make wealth, then they sacrifice their wealth in order to get back their health"
– Dalai Lama

Ask yourself these four questions:

- How much time do you spend with family?
- Do you have habits that need to be changed?
- Are you the one who makes decisions when buying groceries?
- What is your favorite physical activity?

You may notice a pattern in these questions.

Right now, at this very unique time, your answers probably differ from 2 months ago, but the overall direction is the same – they are all about health.

Health and time - these two treasures are given to us to cherish over a lifetime, and cannot be replenished or replaced. We can buy just about everything else, but these two - we only get one chance at, and it's up to us how we use it. At this very challenging time, it all comes down to the same very basic principles: move your body, drink more water, get enough sleep and enjoy quality time with your family. Simple does not mean wrong. Now, simple means achievable and empowering.

Only when healthy, will we be able to pursue happiness, take care of others, and make lives easier. And remember – help is available to anyone who asks for it.

Irina Strunina is a Master of Sports and Certified in Nutrition for Heart Disease and Diabetes. Irina uses her passion for health and her experience in sports and healthy cooking to guide her customers to better health.

https://www.facebook.com/irina.strunina

Rusty Ethics? Dirty Tactics? Spring Clean Your Business!

Rusty Ethics? Dirty Tactics? Spring Clean Your Business!

Annie P. Ruggles

"We can't take any credit for our talents. It's how we use them that counts." — Madeleine L'Engle, A Wrinkle in Time

If you've begun to suspect your blood, sweat and tears are leading you away from your voice, dreams, and heart instead of closer to them; it's time to brush up your integrity and your offerings with a Small Business Spring Cleaning!

What are you assuming your clients know about you, your values, and your VALUE?

What industry standards shouldn't be standard for you?

How does it feel, in your body, when you act outside of your integrity?

When was the last time you had that feeling? What triggered it?

When have your mentors or advisors misled you? What lousy advice are you still following?

When is the customer completely wrong? What boundaries do they violate?

What do your competitors do that ruffles your feathers? How can you take a bolder stance against this behavior and actively choose the opposite?

What are you going to stop doing or delegate? Where can you create freedom and lightness?

What processes/offerings/language/images just aren't working anymore? What feels stale? What can and should you eliminate?

What goals have you outgrown? What dreams are struggling to grow, in their shadow?

How can your business be a louder, bolder, braver extension of your heart?

Annie P. Ruggles (Dean of the Non-Sleazy Sales Academy) has guided hundreds of people toward making deeper connections, lasting impressions, and friendlier, more lucrative transactions and conversations.

www.anniepruggles.com

Reflection through Crisis

Reflection through Crisis

Azmina Ahamed

"This time forces us to evaluate having personal breakthroughs so that you can come back even better"

This to me is much more than just a disease. We are all going through a collective grief for what we thought was the normal way of life. Wondering how and if my business will be able to sustain itself and how will I be able to move through during this period.

We can choose to stay in anxiety and fear or we can look at this as an opportunity to reinvent ourselves. We have all been forced to stop!

Time to Re-evaluate, Re-structure, Re-visit, Re-Focus and press the Mindset Reset Button.

Deepening our own practice of faith and leaning into trust and know that what is happening is just the way it's supposed to.

The ability to weather this storm is to be able to tap in to the embodiment of yourself. This means working on your Emotional, Spiritual, Mental, and Physical self. When you pass this crisis you will be able to put the right energy and momentum in your business. Everyone in this world is going through their own personal growth at this time. Coming from a place of compassion, connection, and re-invention will set you apart in your business.

Azmina Ahamed offers tools to manage life in a personal and professional environment. Supporting in the areas of Spiritual, Mental, Emotional and Physical self to achieve our best and happy version.

www.azminaahamed.com

Mindset

Mindset

Barbara Ayers

"Mindfulness is simply being aware of what is happening right now, without wishing it were different. Enjoying the pleasant without holding on when it changes, which it will. Being with the unpleasant without fearing it will always be this way, which it won't." James.Baraz.

Mindset, What does this mean? Our minds are a wonderful creation.

The Brain processes so many thoughts. What do we put into our brains? Mostly trivia.

If only we could set our minds into action, and to see the power it gives us. However, so often we disregard this power, by batting away this precious gift, we have been given. We worry about non-essential things that whirl around in our brain and we come no closer to a solution.

So how do we set our MINDSET IN MOTION? The first thing we must learn is how to let the mind relax. This isn't easy as we have to stop worrying about minor worries or concerns.

We have to find a way to think positively. To stop prodding our minds with unnecessary worries, that block our minds from achieving positive results.

We create obstacles for ourselves, so that the mind cannot fulfil its potential. So, we must learn to relax. Clear our minds of all the clutter.

Choose a quiet place, where you can be alone, and let your mind concentrate on finding you the right path to follow.

With MINDFULNESS, ask yourself what it is that you want to achieve. What is your goal? How to make your business grow and make profits. How to structure your life, so you have constantly got your head down, and feel drained and like you're stuck and getting nowhere. Relaxing the mind takes time to learn, to let your mind do the work.

Our Mind, our brain is so amazing, that if we can learn to let it guide us the results can be formidable. Establish what you want from life, and let your MINDSET do the work.

The mind is so powerful, you will be astonished at the results you can attain. With the present situation, when we are all having to stay indoors, what better time, to put your mind into action. You will be surprised at what you, yes you, can achieve.

Barbara Ayers, who lives in North Somerset, has a lifetime experience of supporting others. As a mother and grandmother, aged 78, She has enjoyed working with children, in the preschool setting, Breakfast Clubs, and After-School clubs for 23 years.

C.P.R Your Creativity.

C.P.R Your Creativity.

Caroline Esterson & Wendy Gannaway

"Creativity is inventing, experimenting, growing, taking risks, breaking rules, making mistakes, and having fun"
Mary Lou Cook

Our world is moving so fast. Perhaps you're filled with terror or have decided to dig deep and get resourceful. Whichever response you have, there is no time like now to get creative.

Creativity is about finding new connections in what is already there. We all have this capability if we are prepared to learn.

At Genius Learning we encourage people to do this through **C.P.R.**

People consume **CONTENT**. They put it into practice or simply load it into their brain and forget it quickly.

We urge people to deepen their learning by exploring the **PROCESS** too; how the content is being delivered. Which personal skills can you enhance through the process (like collaboration, problem solving and decision making).

Then, to strengthen your personal understanding, learn from your **RESPONSE** to the learning. Did you enjoy it or not? What did you find valuable? What does that little voice in your head tell you about your experience?

Remember learning is all around you, in every moment, of every day. When you harness the power of C.P.R. you will start to make connections that will help you pivot to create value in today's new normal.

Caroline Esterson & Wendy Gannaway are on a mission to humanise the workplace in this digitally driven age. We provide learning that drives a culture of collaboration to reduce complexity.

www.inspireyourgenius.com

Be a Webinar Rockstar!

Be a Webinar Rockstar!

Helen Vandenberghe

"Don't be paralysed; just get started." -Leah Schothorst

Teaching your expertise online through webinars, Facebook Lives or Youtube videos can be a fantastic way to pivot your business and reach clients all over the world. However, as more people than ever start using video conferencing tools, doing it professionally can really make you stand out. Here's a few tips to help you shine online.

- If on camera - choose your location carefully (no piles of laundry in the background)!
- Plan your content - don't 'wing it'
- Have one key outcome for your webinar - is the aim to educate, sell or invite to a call?
- Start with a story & grab and hold your audience's attention
- Maintain a conversational tone - no one likes a lecture
- Choose powerful images for your slides (not too busy with words - no one reads them)!
- Use interesting real facts and examples to support your message
- Remember that your voice is the connection - vary your tone, pace and volume for more engagement
- Practice, practice, practice!

Helen Vandenberghe helps coaches and entrepreneurs become successful, published authors, in-demand speakers and high end course creators. Join her fabulous community for free training, tips and opportunities at

https://www.facebook.com/groups/clientattractionnow/.

Be Clear About Your True Purpose in Life

Be Clear About Your True Purpose in Life

Carol Davies

"Shoot for the stars. You are so very important. This changing world needs your ideas, skills, caring, and love. Go out and succeed!"

You hear a lot about getting clarity about yourself, your career and other aspects of your life. So, what is this buzzword 'clarity' and why is it important to have in your life? Simply put, 'clarity' is about getting clear about what is important in your life, what drives you to act and succeed. It has a lot to do with finding your purpose in life.

Do you question your life path, passions, hopes and dreams? Are you saying, "My life's not going where I want it to go, I must not be good enough, I want to give up." or "I know this is what I should be doing but I spend SO much time and energy and am not seeing the results I want". Every time you step into self-doubt, you give away your power. You literally manifest your struggle even more.

Look at your strengths, interests, talents, what gets you excited to go out to work. Be in a quiet place, write down what excites you in life, who you admire and why. What are you good at? These answers will show you the way to a wonderful new life.

Carol Davies is a certified coach, was a manager for many years in the United Nations. She provides leadership training so you can be the best you can be.

www.thepassionmotivator.com

How not to Eat the House When Working From Home!

How not to Eat the House When Working from Home!

Carol May

"When you arise in the morning think of what a precious privilege it is to be alive - to breathe, to think, to enjoy, to love." - Marcus Aurelius

During the recent 'lockdown' period, our world changed.

We felt our health was in danger, being outside felt unsafe, and we felt stressed, anxious and fearful.

This fear is the cue for our reptilian brain to take charge, because we are hard wired for it to do so when our very existence feels threatened.

You may have found yourself feeling out of control around food, the food we have stockpiled for fear it might run out, and you may have been craving carbs, sugar and comfort foods. If we are carrying extra fat, we can't die if food becomes scarce! Simple.

As you're reading this, I hope your life is becoming less restrictive, however, any time we experience rapid change, and increased stress, the same feelings can emerge.

However, we CAN stay safe without eating the house and putting on weight, provided we make some simple changes.

1. Avoid mindless eating and snacking! If you are constantly in the kitchen, ask yourself if you are physically hungry before you start eating chocolate!

2. Plan your meals ahead of time and only buy those ingredients.

3. Take time to prepare your meals with care and eat slowly and mindfully.

4. Don't eat in front of the TV or at your desk.

5. Drink water! 2-3 litres a day preferably.

6. If you need help, ask for it.

Carol May is a Disruptive Health Coach who helps midlife professional women to drop multiple clothes sizes by ditching dieting forever and reconnecting with their body.

www.facebook.com/allshapesandsizessolutions

Don'T Stop Selling!

Don't Stop Selling!

Helen Vandenberghe

'Being good is good business'. Dame Anita Roddick

Maybe you've seen the social media posts urging that online marketers stop promoting their services, and just 'put things on hold', and give away their stuff for free? Because everyone is struggling right now, and no one has any money, right?

I disagree.

Not because I'm a cold-hearted person - but because WE are the economy. And I believe those that CAN sell their services 'virtually' or in a safe, responsible way should. It serves no-one for us ALL to go out of business.

Yes, provide free resources, yes pivot your offers, yes volunteer, and support your community - but if at all possible please don't stop selling. The world needs leaders right now and someone needs your skills.

You've probably also hired dozens of freelancers to support your business over the years - they have families and bills to pay too. I take it as a personal responsibility to stay in business for them.

So if you feel a bit weird about 'selling' when you know that other people are struggling right now, that just means you're human. You have a heart. You also have a business.

Adjust your offer, be more flexible on payment plans, and re-work your packages. There are people who need what you have and DO see the value in it.

Helen Vandenberghe is known as the mentor to rising stars. She helps coaches and entrepreneurs become successful, published authors, in-demand speakers and high-end course creators. Discover how to reinvent your business at her facebook group at:

https://www.facebook.com/groups/clientattractionn ow/

Breathe Your Way to Better.

Breathe Your Way to Better.

Naómi Martell-Bundock

"Take back control of your life instead of letting life control you." Naomi Martell-Bundock.

In times of crisis, we "rise" to the challenge – whatever that may be.

If you have a clearer focus and get a lot done, that's useful, but what if you feel worry or panic? Stress hormones coursing unchecked through our system runs us down, resulting in being a little cranky or feeling low. We might still be delivering high output, but somehow, we're slightly off the mark. (Hopefully someone who loves you, maybe yourself, will highlight this quickly!)

Whether you've been extra focused or anxious, your body and mind need to rest and recuperate so that you can find a sustainable way to be.

~ Pause ~ Stop! ~ Breathe ~ Deeply breathe ~ Repeat ~~ Pause ~ Stop! ~ Breathe ~ Deeply breathe ~ Repeat ~

Conscious breathing helps in minutes. Make it central to your self-care routine.

Practice it twice during the day and in bed at night.

Once you are calm take a moment, a long moment, and consciously choose what you want now.

- What's your aim?
- What will it do for you?
- How do you want to feel generally?

From this centred point, enjoy your conscious action.

Naomi Martell-Bundock has been coaching capable, stressed people to find their own wisdom since 2003. Her website, **www.coresense.co.uk,** offers advice for you personally, as a parent and in your business.

You Never Know Who's Waiting in the Wings.

You Never Know Who's Waiting in the Wings.

Danielle Haley

"There is no power for change greater than a community discovering what it cares about." – Margaret J. Wheatley

When business is slow and the future feels uncertain, focus on bringing value to your online community.

Stay relevant and visible by sharing tips, advice, stories and insights via your website and your social media channels.

Be interesting. Be authoritative. Get creative. Show up day after day with something new to say, and make it impossible for your connections to forget you. Then, when things pick up again – which they inevitably will – you'll be the first in line for new opportunities from followers who have been silently planning, fervently dreaming, and consistently absorbing your content.

Danielle is a copywriter with a strong background in SEO. She creates compelling, search-friendly website content for businesses that take their digital presence seriously. Visit **https://www.indy-consultancy.co.uk**

Meditation to help you to move through obstacles

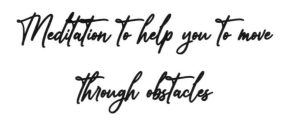

Meditation to help you to move through obstacles

Genny Sapiro

"Meditation and concentration are the way to a life of serenity."– Baba Ram Dass

When life is challenging, and the world seems to be changing so quickly, it can be hugely unsettling, and difficult to come to terms with this 'new normal'

We sometimes need to create our own sense of calm and stability.

This is where meditation can help.

I am an ordained Buddhist disciple and our teachings are transmitted from an enlightened Buddha. Our meditations work on mantra, mudra and visualisation. This helps to purify the mind body and speech.

Here are some tips to get your started:

Make time for you - 10 minutes a day.

Start before you rise or as you fall asleep, if there's barely time in the day.

Play some lovely meditation music.

Light some incense and a candle.

Sit comfortably and relax. Shut your eyes. Be mindful of your breath as you take a few deep breaths in and out.

Genny Sapiro is an ordained Buddhist disciple, a clairvoyant medium and has been working in this field for many lifetimes. She found her calling 10 years ago. It was her lifeline to help others and combine her clairvoyant skills to help people with their karmas that can be causing blocks. Contact Genny at: **Gensapiro@icloud.com**

Color Your World with Happiness!

Color Your World with Happiness!

Barbara Ellison

"Challenges are part of life. How you handle them is totally up to you. Will you use them to strengthen your character or let them defeat your dreams?"

A friend of mine once asked a question that forever changed my life.

It was a simple question, "what do you want?" My answer was equally simple, yet profound. "I just want people to be happy".

That has become my mission, to be in search of happiness, so that happiness is the norm, not the exception, in people's lives.

Too often we are waiting for our circumstances to change to find our happiness, when I lose 30 pounds, when my husband/wife retires, when I have a six-figure income and the list goes on.

When I woke up from my widow's fog, I knew I wanted to find happiness again...but I didn't know yet how to get there. What I did know was that I had to find out who I was as a person?

That became step one of my five-point method to get your happy back.

Who are you and what do you want?

The only one who can answer those 2 questions is you, and the only place to find those answers is deep within yourself.

For myself, I meditated every morning. That quiet space got me then, and now, every day, in touch with myself and that makes me happy.

Barbara Ellison is a woman who has been divorced, widowed and bankrupted. Barbara knows the value of personal happiness & how personality impacts communication. She is a Certified Trainer & Happiness Coach. Visit Barbara at:

http://www.movingonmovement.com/home/

Reweave the Narrative

Reweave the Narrative

Alison Haitana

"As a bee gathering nectar does not harm or disturb the colour & fragrance of the flower; so do the wise move through the world." – Gautama Buddha

The power of language is all around us. This is why it is imperative that we are discerning and careful about what we let into our internal spaces. More importantly, we need to exercise diligence in the language we use to describe our self, our feelings and experiences.

One phrase that helps me immensely in challenging internal and external times is the following;

This is happening FOR me, not TO me.

A simple phrase, that has within it a spaciousness that allows me to breathe, sit and reflect on what is. More importantly, my personality isn't in a reactive state. I am given time and energy to come up with creative solutions. One where miracles can be created and new ideas have a chance to gestate and see the light of day.

By allowing this phrase to enter my life, I throw myself a lifeline and drop the victim mentality. I am allowing myself to embrace a more expansive and universal mindset.

In allowing myself this gift of language, I am able to see opportunities and areas where I can grow my soul strength. Becoming more resilient and aware in the process.

This is my gift for you also.

Alison Haitana is a Shamaness, Intuitive Healer and StoryWeaver. Alison also loves to support heart centered, creative and spiritual entrepreneurs with Intentional Creativity sessions to unlock your visionary self.

www.alchemicalrainbow.com

Be The Phoenix!

Be The Phoenix!

Alison Thomson

"Carpe diem"
"Seizing the day with head, hands and heart has never been truer than in a time of crisis!"

At a time of crisis so much is out of your control, it is easy to be swept along by the wave of panic.

You are probably right, there is a lot happening that you cannot control. But this is the moment to change your course amid this stream.

Take back your power, and see the possibilities in what you can control. Find the positives, they are usually there just not always easy to spot.

Liberating your psychological, emotional and creative headspace will free you up to see the opportunities beyond the threat. Truly open yourself up to the personal and business opportunities that might come maybe in the threat itself or in the period after the crisis. And don't feel guilty this doesn't make you a vulture, feeding off others' difficulties.

Being the phoenix does not have to be at the expense of others.

Alison Thomson is known as The Safety Elf. She is passionate about making a difference to peoples' health safety and wellbeing. She loves exploding expectations about 'elf and safety, engaging people and making it fun. Visit Alison at: **www.thesafetyelf.co.uk**

Keep on (Self)-Promoting Even in Uncertain Times

Keep on (Self)-Promoting Even in Uncertain Times

Amanda Fitzgerald

"Share what you do with the world, we need you more than ever!"

On New Year's Eve 2020, we all welcomed in the New Year and New Decade with open arms as we resolved to make 2020 our best year ever and that 2020 and beyond would be where our businesses flourished and grew beyond our wildest dreams.

Everything was really appearing to be going so well to plan. Then this global crisis hit and words like unprecedented, challenging, pivot became used and overused, for good reason.

I coach entrepreneurs to get press coverage so that they can share their message with millions as they create an impact on the world.

Even in uncharted and unprecedented times we don't stop making an impact, we still have incredible messages to share in our local communities or much further afield.

People still need our services, and WE NEED YOU!

So, it is not the time to put the brakes on. It's not the time to hide. It's the time more than ever to be super visible and to share what you do, because if you don't, then who else will do it for you?

And as for the P word...pivot: I challenge you to pivot from keeping invisible to self-promoting. You will be thanked for it. Just remember the 80/20 rule in communication: 80% helping others out / 20% self-promotion.

You can do it. Make 2020 your year to pivot to promote.

Amanda FitzGerald is known as The Ultimate Door Opener as she coaches her clients on how to pitch to long sought-after journalists and influencers.

www.amandapr.com

Step Up From The Energy Of Despair

Step Up From The Energy Of Despair

Marianne Dupuis Janin

"Tap into your inner anger source and you will thrive in most meaningful ways."

All human beings facing crisis experience fear: this is our inherent human condition, no shame to have. Unfortunately, we may then easily slip into paralysis and discouragement. If we want to thrive, we need to go beyond this fear, to the other side and place where we find courage and action.

Where to find that source of energy to thrive?

Consider a situation that shocks you intensely, something disastrous that needs to stop now, or it will dramatically hurt people who truly matter to you. Just thinking about it will generate your inner anger and from this source will grow your hunger for action.

For me, what is truly shocking is wasting your amazing talents for lack of emotional intelligence. Reigning by fear while fostering potential could reach rocket results.

So, leverage this energy of despair and you will have no other choice but to step up and keep going no matter what. From that place your courage will grow and contribute to make significant positive changes. Tap into your inner anger source and you will thrive in most meaningful ways.

Marianne Dupuis helps executives with high turnover in their teams to become leaders people seek to work for, with teams thriving despite cultural differences. Download her complimentary Effective Feedback guide. Here :

https://sendfox.com/lp/3lyklm

You Got This! No Matter What!

You Got This! No Matter What!

Valerie Dwyer

"When you have a Powerful, Exciting and Crystal-Clear Vision for How You Can Create Your Life and Your World, Everything Changes. And THAT'S When the Magic Happens!"

You CAN do this! Opportunities are everywhere, if you would only see them.

With 30 years' experience, 10 businesses and three recessions behind me, I help business owners like you navigate choppy waters, breakthrough barriers and rise to reinvent.

You've had the busy, busy and done the outer work.

Now do the inner work for you, which is more sustainable and lasts for life.

Your perfect formula is: Motivate your mindset and master mindful meditation (silence your inner critic). Clear Your Mind Clutter (opens your creative brain space for new ideas). Vitalise your Values (stops sabotage - self and others).

Visualise your Vital Vision Blueprint™, (switch on your success 'SatNav' to spot those opportunities that are right for you as you traverse your roadmap to your ideal life and business).

Manifest your magnificent Masterplan.

Act with accountability (self and others) and arrive exactly where you want to be when this time passes, as it surely will! Remember these three things. Mindset Matters because your thoughts become things. Make them constructive. Your beliefs affect everything you are, do and have. Positives attract and negatives deflect.

When you are down, the ONLY way is up.

Valerie Dwyer is an Award Winning Success Coach and Mentor. Valerie helps ambitious, successful business owners rebuild confidence, gain clarity, focus and direction, generate growth ideas and break through barriers to greater success.

valerie@mywonderfullifecoach.co.uk

Why Sleep is Vital to your Well-Being

Why Sleep is Vital To your Well-Being

Amanda O'Rourke

"As important as it is to have a plan for doing work, it is perhaps more important to have a plan for rest, relaxation, self-care, and sleep." Akiroq Brost.

The quantity of sleep you get each night is crucial to your well-being. Eight hours is the recommended amount for adults. The quality of sleep is also vital. There are three sleep stages: light, deep and rapid eye movement (REM).

If the body is sleep deprived, it will revert to light sleeping only. Deep sleep, also known as "beauty sleep", is essential for cell repair and renewal. REM sleep is vital for cognitive functions, such as learning and memory recall.

When stressed, you might find yourself sleep deprived.

If you struggle to get off to sleep at night, keep a pen and pad by your bedside and make a note of your worries and promise yourself you will consider them the next day.

If you wake during the night, according to Prof Steve Peters, author of 'The Chimp Paradox', the limbic area of your brain awakens first. This "chimp" brain activates our fight, flight or freeze responses. This explains why our fears feel worse in the small hours!

If you acknowledge that the logical, reasoning, "human" part of your brain is not yet awake, you can resolve to think through solutions in the morning when things will inevitably look better.

Amanda O'Rourke is a coach, who helps business owners live a more abundant life. She is also a certified Youth Mental Health First Aider and mentor for The Girls' Network.

www.happycoach.co.uk

Live Your Own Life, Not Someone Else's

Live Your Own Life, Not Someone Else's

Rachel Smets

"You are the editor of your own life. Change your life by changing the stories you tell yourself."

"Beauty begins the moment YOU decide to tell your OWN story." This quote from Coco Chanel describes how important it is to STOP comparing yourself to others, and be the best version of yourself.

Let me ask you: Are you living YOUR life, or someone else's? In other words, are you living the life you're meant to live, or are you doing what you think you ''should'' be doing for others?

It's completely human to compare, especially with social media, scrolling through images of dream holidays, seemingly perfect relationships, amazing fit bodies or fabulous achievements.

We are fooled to believe others' lives are better than ours.

We are fooled to believe the grass is greener on the other side.

Everyone has bad days!

It's time to STOP comparing and start telling your OWN story.

Look at yourself, hold up a mirror and realize all the things you DO have, not the things you lack.

Look at others to be inspired and find out what you can learn from them so you can grow and develop yourself.

You are unique!

You are in control of your own life. Live Life without regrets!

Tell me: What's your story?

Rachel Smets is a Clarity coach, TEDx speaker, Author, YouTuber, teacher. She helps ambitious professionals to build your dream life, not someone else's. Find Clarity, Confidence and Create your next step to the life you desire.

https://www.rachelsmets.com/

3 Steps to Ensure Your Marketing Is Effective!

3 Steps To Ensure Your Marketing Is Effective!

Regina Bergman

"So many of our dreams at first seem impossible, then, they seem improbable, and then, when we summon the will, they soon become inevitable." - Christopher Reeve

You have just published your marketing piece and are now waiting for the sales to roll in. Wrong!!! Marketing is not responsible for sales but for generating leads! If done properly, you will be attracting prospects to you so that you can make the sale.

Here are the 3 things to know and understand about what marketing should do:

1. Grab the reader's attention. If it doesn't, it is worthless. When you're communicating with your prospects, the "headline" is your bold claim.

2. Facilitate their information gathering and decision-making process. No matter who they are or what they're buying, they are looking for the best deal (VALUE). That doesn't mean lowest price...it means the most value for the price. They will pay a higher price for increased value.

3. Your marketing must contain a low, or no risk offer to further facilitate their decision-making process. You

have to give them a compelling...yet safe way to take the next step. That next step may be to buy what you sell if you sell a lower priced product or service. If you sell high ticket items, that next step may be to simply request additional information.

Regina Bergman is an International Best-Selling Author, Public Speaker, Marketing Strategist and Business Growth Specialist. She helps transform businesses, both online and offline, while helping entrepreneurs realize their vision of positively impacting lives.

BridgeportIsMarketing.com

Maintain your Balance through Chaos with Meditation

Maintain your Balance through Chaos with Meditation

Lynette Allen

"It's time for you to meet the calm, to distance yourself from chaos, go inwards and focus on that place within you where calm resides."

I've learned that there will always be chaos. That life can be chaos! One moment it's still and peaceful, the next it's different and crazy, but WE don't have to be different and crazy. It's possible to accept the chaos, to ride it, like choppy seas. We never expect the sea to be calm all the time, we know that storms and thunder, lightning and rough seas are part of the movement of the planet. Through physical and mindful stillness we ride those waves with grace and emotional stability.

Calm and balance is not outside of ourselves, but inside. Deep, deep inside. Distance yourself from chaos by sitting. Close your eyes. Breathe. Don't time it, don't set an alarm. Just sit physically still and breathe. Breathe in. Breathe out. Open the window. Listen to the birds. Hear the silence. Hear your breath. Focus inwards, on the air in your lungs, moving gently in and out until your mind settles. Allow all your thoughts to settle to the floor of your mind. Stay physically still, breathe and you will meet your calm - the calm that is in you consistently. It's time for you to meet the calm.

Lynette Allen; Medicine Woman, author & broadcaster. She swapped corporate life for the jungle, holding sacred space

for women; serving Cacao and honouring them with ritual and ceremony.
www.awomansblessing.com

Creating Habits that Serve, Rather than Sell

Creating Habits that Serve, Rather than Sell

LaFaye Pye

"We have to think, believe, act-upon and manage our time, emotions, habits and finances in both the best of times and in the worst of times."

We all have personal stories of success and failure.

We all shall be born, live and die.

We eat, wear clothes and need shelter.

We love and are loved.

We create communities, cultivate friendships and raise families.

These are the things that tie us together as humans beings.

But, somewhere in the middle, is where we find and create our ideal life. It's where legacies are formed and legends live on.

Unfortunately, courage doesn't come from happiness. It's formed and developed through challenges, failure and difficult times. From the darkness we find strength, passion, purpose and true meaning in our lives.

Only then do we come to realize just how bright our love, kindness and consideration of others can shine. And this my friend, is the secret key to success in difficult times….

It's helping others, and in helping others you help yourself! After all, if you "help enough people to get what they want, you will surely get what you want." - Zig Ziglar

Serve, be the best version of you.

Create habits daily, comfort and uplift others.

People may forget what you said, but they will never forget how you made them feel.

Be the best version of you.

LaFaye Pye is the founder of Business Builders Lab. She helps women-pereneurs create financial independence online. Her Plan, Build and Launch Method streamlines businesses. Eliminating anxiety and overwhelm. Replacing them with courage, confidence and consistent cash-flow.

www.BusinessBuildersLab.com

Stop & Focus ONLY on What You Want!

Stop & Focus ONLY on What You Want!

Rosemary Cunningham

"Think of the feeling of creating what you want. It feels like love! And get excited. Excitement and positive expectation help us create much quicker!"

I've had to reinvent my business several times and have helped many clients do the same when work has disappeared overnight.

In the panic, it can be tempting to freeze or to take the first opportunity that comes along to just get money in the bank. These decisions are made from fear, reaction and are rarely the best path for us. It's important to take time to stop, feel the feelings, reflect and ask yourself these two questions.

1. Why do I do what I do? If nothing else was left, what's important, what makes your soul sing?
2. Who am I in my business and who do I love to be?

Be crystal clear on the feeling of your big why. Keeping that in your thoughts allows the Reticular Activating System, the matchmaker in your brain to dutifully show you more of what you are thinking, feeling and focussing on.

So, to attract new opportunities that light you up, keep your focus only on what you want to create in your life. Direct your thoughts and your RAS will show you opportunities that match and then it's up to us to follow the breadcrumbs! Focus only on what you want!

Rosemary Cunningham specialises in helping women find their soul's purpose, attract ideal clients and find the perfect marketing for their business which attracts those clients with grace and ease.

www.rosemarycunningham.co.uk

Create Your Protection Bubble!

Create Your Protection Bubble!

Sarah Brunel-while & Helen Vandenberghe

'If you hold yourself dear, protect yourself well.'
Gautama Buddha

During tough times, you may find yourself surrounded by more negativity than usual. Maybe it's the constant news on TV, maybe you're receiving endless phone calls from worried and anxious friends, or maybe you're spending much more time with challenging family members than you usually would?

One visualization technique that can be helpful is to create a 'protection bubble'!

Just as we put on clothes to protect our body and carry an umbrella in the rain, we can step into our projection bubble to protect our energy.

Every morning, imagine you are stepping in to a huge bubble extending about six inches all around you. To reinforce this imagine, picture someone running at you and bouncing off (and yes you can laugh at that!).

Know that in your bubble you are safe, confident and strong. Nothing anyone else says or does can affect you. As you go through your day, if you come across negativity, just visualize it 'bouncing off your bubble'!

It may seem silly– but even if you just giggle at the thought of this, you will have changed your mental and physical state.

You can also imagine you are holding a shield, like a powerful action hero! Children have no problem thinking they are superheroes with super powers. Maybe we could learn a thing or two from them!

Sarah Brunel-while has been a holistic therapist for over 25 years. She has studied, sports & remedial massage & more recently, hypnotherapy. With a past as an accomplished ice dancer & having beaten cancer, she knows about regaining your balance and recovering from falls and setbacks!

She loves supporting women & men to feel more confident within their own skin, and empowering people to discover their inner strength.

Helen Vandenberghe helps coaches and entrepreneurs become successful, published authors, in-demand speakers and high end course creators. She's been friends with Sarah for over a decade. Visit. **www.writeyourbook.biz**

The World Needs You

The World Needs You

Sandra Noble

"Note to Self: The world needs you to show up today. You are powerful. You are valuable & what you believe changes the world." - Samantha Hammack

There is nothing I have to do to be valuable and worthwhile. I just have to be. I've discovered: Who I am is more than enough. Even when I procrastinate. Even when I make mistakes. Even when I fail.

Failure is just a label we put on ourselves. Despite the outcome, we are a success for attempting and risking. What other labels and beliefs do you need to shed that are holding you back? Beliefs like "I'm worthless, "The world is scary" or "I don't deserve". Let them all go! Forgive yourself!

God acts through us. You are the one that can give a smile. You are the one that can visit the sick. You are the one with the infectious laugh. You are the one with the calming effect. You are the one with the great insight.

My purpose is to express God as only I can. And God needs you to serve the world as only you can. As long as we have breath in our bodies, we are needed, valuable and important to the mosaic of the universe. As Rickie Byars says in her song "Use Me", the world needs us to shine. Be perfectly you.

Sandra Noble has been an IT professional for 30+ years and a multi-preneur. Currently owns b2b marketing agency, Noble Wise Marketing. At 70 I am embracing my wisdom and resiliency.
https://www.linkedin.com/in/SandraNoble/

You + Numerology = Business Success

You + Numerology = Business Success

Jo Soley

"The flip side to being restricted on movement is that we have the time to do the things we have wanted to do for ages …"

Numerology is the science, philosophy and psychology of life interpreted from the symbols of names, dates and numbers. We are all named, coded, numbered and placed in the great eternal plan.

Numerology gives you another way of doing things, a clearer path in which to head. Using numerology guides you, helping you understand yourself at a deeper level.

Numerology brings Aha! moments related to what is currently going on in your business and assists in opening doors to possibilities. Numerology shows us not only personality analysis but how we can make better business decisions.

Knowing your personal numbers can assist you in these uncertain times - helping you be resilient, helping you strive in times of stress and helping you understand how to manage stress.

Bizology is not maths or statistics! It's spiritual empowerment into business, aligning your business vision with your personality.

Let me show you a treasure map not a business plan! Find out your numbers below.

Jo Soley is a marketing and business coach and the founder of Bizology - helping you use the powers of numerology to elevate your business success. Visit Jo online **HERE. (https://bit.ly/3bg7yXY)**

Time to Reflect

Time to Reflect

Anna-Maria Hawke

"Self-motivation, energy and resilience."

So, this recent situation has made us all stop. Each and every one of us affected so how can we mentally manage this?

See it as an opportunity for reflection. Do I want to go back to normal? What's my normal and is it working for me? So, I start with my usual self-care, get up early, look at the morning and go for a long walk with the sausage dog in tow. Being out in nature always energises me and gives me clarity. I work through my thoughts and start to figure things out.

I come home, I bake, I experiment with something new and think about overhauling my whole afternoon tea menu. It feels therapeutic and creative. For me, food has always meant love so I think about how I can translate this in my future business plans. What is the essence of my business? I want to create a wonderful experience. I want to surround people with beautiful things, feed them and let them feel cared for. This time gives me the opportunity to really understand myself, my motivations and my drivers and confirms that my whole business really is just an extension of me.

Anna-Maria Hawke combined her love of all things vintage with her passion for baking and creating beautiful things. From a kitchen table business in 2010 to hosting vintage styled events for 350 guests. **www.veryvintageteaparty.net**

What you Focus On,
Consumes your Thoughts

What you Focus On, Consumes your Thoughts

Shalini Menezes

"God has brought us through and He will bring us through again, Make a decision each day, to choose faith over fear."

In today's world, we are inundated from everywhere with news. Some of it elevates our mood, some of us drives us down to our lowest low. Others bring in a feeling that life is still beautiful and the best of all makes us realize that we are humans and humanity every time is always a given.

As we tune our minds and eyes to focus on the happenings around the world, let us choose the rights ones that will help us feel good – it doesn't mean we let go of the alarming issues that are garnering importance – every single piece of news was created with an intent – for the writer and the viewer – It can create Fear or elevate our Faith – the choice is ours and it is Faith in ourselves and the universe.

Focusing on the right F, will surely help us wade through these times when we are instructed by our government authorities to stay home, we need to follow these instructions and whilst at home thanks to technology, let's tap into hidden talents that were lost in the layers of our busy lives, unfurl them, swirl with joy with the right 'F' Faith in ourselves :)

Shalini Menezes is a wife, a mom, a working woman, a poet, a passionate toastmaster, and a regular contributor for leading newspapers in Dubai.
https://thinkrightfeellight.wordpress.com/

When Life Tumbles In

When Life Tumbles In

Teresa Blount

"It is in the throes of adversity that we exchange our rights for privileges"

In times of uncertainty when life seems to tumble in, the tendency can be to retreat...

Instead of spinning in anxiety and worry, it's vital to focus on the things we can control.

In these times more than ever, it is important to take care of our body, mind and spirit and focus on finding the opportunity for joy, grace, and tenderness with ourselves and others.

Find the strength that comes out of struggle. Understand the power we have to make change for the better...

The following suggestions can empower growth through challenging times:

1. Bookend the day. Begin each day on purpose. Have a consistent morning and evening routine. View evening as the beginning of the next day.

2. Use words that empower and inspire. The words you choose have voltage.

3. Stand tall. Breathe deep. Meditate. Pray. During times of chronic stress health plummets.

4. Focus on eating plenty of fresh fruits and vegetables.

5. Hydrate well. Plenty of good clean water to flush toxins and regulate blood pressure.

6. Get good, deep sleep...especially between 10 p.m. and 2 a.m.

7. Go easy on the people around you. Keep your hearts, minds, and arms wide open. Love yourself, others, and life more.

Teresa Blount is an LPC in mental health and psychology. She is trained as a coach in high-performance habits and formerly owned a music school and a private counseling practice.

https://bit.ly/3cbKLhi

Spiritual Mind Treatment boost for good Mental Health

Spiritual Mind Treatment boost for good Mental Health

Vatsala Shukla

These are difficult times for all of us and it's easy to fall into the trap of negative thinking or thought patterns that impact our mental health.

There is a way to eliminate negative thought patterns within our personal subconscious mind through sublimation by the Higher Mind or God-Mind within ourselves.

Known as Spiritual Mind Treatment in metaphysical science, this is actually prayer!

30 years ago I intuitively developed a 5 minute mini-prayer for times when I felt a sense of negativity and needed to return to my Source to center myself.

My technique enables me to make better choices, decisions and handle crisis with calmness.

Here's the technique.

Sit cross legged with your index finger touching your thumb in both hands and visualize yourself surrounded by a white protective aura. Start praying to God to give you guidance, clarity on the distressing issue and protection from the evil and negative influences in the environment.

End the prayer with a statement where you place your life and circumstances in God's hand yield to God's better judgment of knowing what's right for you and ask for guidance.

Give yourself this Spiritual Mind Treatment daily and see the difference it makes for you!

Vatsala Shukla is a Best- Selling Author, Change Catalyst, and Career & Business Coach, mentors professionals to achieve their desired career aspirations and authentic life balance.

https://karmicallycoaching.com

Overcome overwhelm with the SoulFire 5D Decision-Making Matrix

Overcome overwhelm with the SoulFire 5D Decision-Making Matrix

Zoe Goode

"It's said that visionary decision making happens at the intersection of intuition and logic, and it's an art only when you don't know the science. But I believe it's both."

We all know overwhelm can be a bitch, keeping us stuck whilst our dreams slowly die inside us.

So, when it feels like you're drowning in your to-do list with no lifeline in sight, use my 5D Decision-Making Matrix to help identify your priorities and take action on the things that matter.

Instinctively assign each of your to-do's one of the five D's and take inspired intentional action!

The 5D's are:

Do it - The important high-priority activities that help you achieve your dreams.

Ditch it - Let go of distractions and things other people want you to do. It's ok to politely decline.

Delegate it - You don't have to do everything yourself. Choose someone to delegate to, hand it over with faith and praise for their expertise and valued support then get back to your priorities.

Delay it - Sometimes if it's worth doing, it's worth doing well. Give items that can wait a date and time when you can commit your full focus and take more effective action later.

Do it less well - I know it sounds horrendous the idea of not giving everything your very best effort. But trust me, it is better than perfect!

Zoe Goode is the Intrepid Leader of The SoulFire Revolution. She's on a mission to ignite the world with intuitive badassery. Fueled by books, bourbon and the belief there's a better way.

www.thesoulfirerevolution.com

Change is Inevitable. Thriving and Growing is Intentional.

Change is Inevitable. Thriving and Growing is Intentional.

Marla Hall

"Every experience is a wellspring of wisdom. Listening with a loving heart, open mind, and expanded awareness imparts the lesson, learning, and gift, henceforth shining a brighter light ahead."

Preparedness complements change, even without knowing when, where, or what might affect you, your business or your loved ones.

Blending inner wisdom, self-care and collaborative relationships generates unlimited options, stimulates resilience, increases flexibility and directs focus to meet any circumstance, any time.

Take Time for You

- How do you pamper yourself?
- Do you take frequent breaks?
- Do you read, play a sport, walk or hike?
- Have you a desire to-do list?

Make Time for Others

- How do you balance work with family, friends, laughter, love, and play for greater productivity and all-around satisfaction?

- Live in community, in-person and online. Play games, watch movies, and enjoy dinner parties.

- Which skills, talents, capabilities, and experience can you offer others? Is there a hidden profit maker?

Spend Time Within

- Communion involves becoming quiet to energize, set or reset.

- Prayer and Meditation are personal, private, and in present time. Call the connection source what you wish. Do it anywhere. Eyes open or closed, with or without a candle or soft music. Stand, sit, or lie down.

Marla Hall has experienced unplanned job loss from burnout, job elimination, and global outsourcing. As a transition coach, author, and speaker, she teaches work-life balance strategies and pre-retirement lifestyle planning.

www.RetireOnFirePlan.com

Create Something Stellar and Sell It

Create Something Stellar and Sell It

Debs de Vries

"...move towards what you truly desire... and your vision becomes clearer." Jesse Lyn Stoner.

Have you noticed the feeling of potential in this time of restrictions?

Ask yourself, "What do I want to be the result of this unique space and time? "

If, like me, you've decided to create something stellar, then I'd like to share my process.

Commit, 100%, from conception to birth. No matter what. Write down your commitment, sign it and get it witnessed! You don't need to know what it is yet.

Get your pens, crayons, notebook; whatever you feel suits you best for initial idea capture. Before you start, sit quietly and draw in some deep slow breaths. When you feel still and centered, just ask yourself:

"How can I serve and feel joy in what I offer?".

Just flow with whatever comes. Capture it all. No second guessing, no restrictions, no judgment. Write, paint, make up extreme situations, be playful.

If you don't see a thread yet, wait. Keep the door in your imagination open.

When you have refined your ideas and feel aligned, check viability. Reach out to at least 5 people (don't email). Find out how they respond to your idea. Keep refining with feedback to guide you.

Debs de Vries offers women a unique path of growth in their perimenopausal years. By uplevelling four key areas - physical, emotional, psychological and spiritual - women unlock the hidden power and direction that is their birthright. **www.debsdevries.com**

Your Soul's Power

Your Soul's Power

Melesha Bailey

"Invest in the human soul. Who knows, it might be a diamond in the rough." - Mary McLeod Bethune

There are times in life when we have no choice but to rise and become our best selves, especially when everything around us is in chaos.

Finding your Soul's Power is finding a path to be better when you have no choice but to soar above limiting beliefs and discover strength in the unknown.

Knowing you are limitless to create a life that is full of meaning and purpose, from the core of your being,

Spend time listening to what your soul is saying to you. Allow your mind to lead you to a place deep within, where there is no fear. You will find the creative power that has been deep down in your soul that's been waiting to emerge.

Your Soul's Power is what will catapult you to emerge as your best self.

Melesha Bailey is a Certified Nutritional Health Coach and Owner of Love 4 Life Wellness. Melesha is a graduate of the Institute of Integrative Nutrition.

www.love4lifewellness.com

Keep Showing Up!

Keep Showing Up!

Helen Vandenberghe

'The power of visibility can never be underestimated'.
Margaret Cho

You may be tempted to hide right now, when things are uncertain and the 'rules of the game' seem to have changed so quickly.

Perhaps you're not sure what you should be selling, or even saying. But if you've had any kind of social media presence for your business before this, then I urge you - keep showing up!

People need leaders especially now. They need encouragement. And they need your skills.

If you're not sure what to say, just ask yourself "What's the best way I can add value today?".

Maybe it's a tip sharing your business expertise, maybe it's a 'behind the scenes' video showing you working from home, maybe it's a funny cat video!

You don't need to have all the answers, or be the 'expert'. But you need to be there. Wherever they normally would 'see' you, and maybe it's time to try a few new things.

Why not;

Host a weekly webinar or 'live'

Guest on podcasts

Write for your local paper

Host an online networking event

Share resources you've discovered

Your voice matters. Use it now.

Helen Vandenberghe is known as the mentor to rising stars. She helps coaches and entrepreneurs become successful, published authors, in-demand speakers and high end course creators. Discover how to reinvent your business at **www.readytorise.co.uk**

Learn To Be Authentic

Learn To Be Authentic

Andrée Funnell

"Understanding yourself is the beginning of all wisdom. You will understand why things are as they are and why your life is as it is!"

When facing challenging times, we can sometimes feel lost, disorientated and pulled in many directions. This is when it is especially helpful to find your own voice and be truly authentic. Here's a few tips to help:

1. Believe in and appreciate yourself

You will never be truly free until you have discovered your authentic self. Whilst you are acting as an imposter, you are holding yourself back from living authentically. Learn to appreciate yourself.

2. Learn from the people you most admire

Think about people in your life who you admire the most i.e. friends, family, your partner, colleagues etc. What traits attract you for instance: Are they considerate? Driven? Forgiving? Mirror the qualities you like and have identified in others.

3. Don't try to please everyone

Stop fretting about what other people are thinking about you. Trying to please everyone is an impossible task as no matter what you do or say there will always be someone out there who will judge you.

4. Detox your relationships and associations

Negative people have negative thoughts which you have no control over. They drain your energy and can be toxic if you allow them to influence you. Exclude them from your life. When working and when online socially, minimise the contact you have with them and be civil.

Andrée Funnell is a multi-award winning Coach/Trainer, author and speaker. Her self-help book is a step by step guide to turning your life around by living authentically.

www.behind-the-mask-book.com

Compare, No! Be Proud, Yes!

Compare, No! Be Proud, Yes!

Cherry-Ann Carew

"Personality begins where comparison leaves off. Be unique. Be memorable. Be confident. Be proud." – Shannon L. Alder.

Comparing yourself to others depletes your confidence, motivation, self-esteem and only serves to get you embroiled in emotional Cha Cha.

The thing is, nearly everyone does it, or has done it, consciously or subconsciously. There are several challenges that occur when you compare yourself to others, because everyone has a different starting point and you can't compare progress, results, or, success unless the starting points are the same; they never are.

Everyone has a different level of talent. Some people are blessed with a high IQ. Others, a natural flair for music or sports...different starting points.

Resources that are available to you may not be to others. For instance, you desire to play the cello. Your mother is a successful international concert cellist hence, you already have an advantage over someone who's family is financially challenged and no one in the family has any musical experience. Again, different starting points.

The best comparison is to your past self. Set a few goals with a timeline and take action towards them each day, then self-reflect. You'll feel proud when you write the pages of your own life, see the progress you've made and can kick those comparative thoughts to the kerb.

Cherry-Ann Carew is an Online Business Coach. She supports emerging business owners simplifying their start-up journey and helps existing businesses scale to the next level. Visit her website at: **https://cherryanncarew.com**

Five Questions Every Intelligent Investor Must Ask

Five Questions Every Intelligent Investor Must Ask

Minesh Baxi

"Every Crisis Has a Lesson"

In the 2007-2008 downturn, I was crushed. My income had gone down by 50%, I had lost money due to bad advice and realized that I had not been saving enough for short term as well as long term needs.

Are you facing any or all of those challenges? Here is some great advice.

Five Questions Every Intelligent Investor Must Ask:

1. Do I just have disparate Investment Products or an overall Investment Strategy?

2. Do I have a strategy to protect money as much as possible from these three -Taxation, Inflation, Market Fluctuation?

3. Does my strategy have these three accounts?

- Short-Term, Mid-Term, Long-Term

4. Am I asking these questions, before making a compelling case for moving money?

- Is my money too exposed to the three things that could

take my money, Taxation, Inflation and Market fluctuation ?

- Does my current money have no strategy? Will my future investment needs be met by implementing a better strategy?

- Are my investment fees too high to justify returns in the current products?

- Are my investment products giving poor performance?

- Am I getting poor service? Like no one is available to answer key questions?

5. Does my strategy include playing Offense and Defense?

Remember, money takes twice as long to come back as it does to go down. We must have a plan to grow our money while protecting it as well.

Minesh Baxi has published 9 books and is focused on coaching business owners to be financially strong.

mbaxi.com/investmentquestions

Dealing with the Emotional Rollercoaster of Change.

Dealing with the Emotional Rollercoaster of Change.

Kerrie Maitland

"Change brings a roller coaster of emotions, accept them and trust that when you are ready you will find strength, clarity and creativity to take the next step."

A change is like riding a rollercoaster; you're anxious, it's something different. The barrier lowers, the ride starts, fear kicks in and your heart falls to your stomach.

Here is how to understand your emotions and create focus in your business when facing uncertainty.

Anxieties are fuelled by unanswered questions. Work with what you know and can control.

- Based on information you know, how will this impact your business?
- How does it change your clients' needs?

When implementing business changes, you may experience fears. Get clear on what is driving them.

- Identify the exact fears; what evidence is there to support them?
- Based on the evidence are modifications necessary?

Frustrations can develop because your clients have other

priorities. Be patient, be visible and when they're ready you will be at the forefront of their minds.

When you hit a low, practice self-care, focus on what is essential and work on building a positive mindset.

- What are the three things to do today?
- What three things are good about today?

As the depression lifts, experiment, what is working and what isn't.

- What further modifications can you integrate?
- How can you prepare your business for the new normal?

(Adapted from Kulber-Ross's Change Curve 1969)

Kerrie Maitland is a career coach focused on empowering women to take control of their careers. Following a successful international HR career of 20 years, she left the corporate world to create a business focusing on empowering women to make career changes with confidence and clarity. **www.positivedimensions.co.uk**

Get Organised — Reduce Overwhelm and Regain Control!

Get Organised – Reduce Overwhelm and Regain Control!

Louise Simpson

"Insanity is doing the same thing over and over again and expecting different results". - Albert Einstein

In times of uncertainty, it is easy to feel like you have no control over anything and that is where overwhelm kicks in – but it really doesn't have to be that way!

By organising your home, you can regain control and give yourself more time to focus on the things that really matter. You can get others in the home involved too – teamwork makes the dream work!

Start with areas you use frequently, such as sorting out your clothes, organising your kitchen drawers or tackling your paperwork pile. The next time you need something, you will save time searching and be able to find it straightaway – giving you more time to get to grips with all of those other things on your to do list!

Categorise – keep like with like and establish files for paperwork, such as home, health, school etc

Declutter – take time to question why you are keeping the item. Will you use it? Does it make you feel good? Or are you only keeping it because you feel like you should?

Organise – now you have the things you want in your home and know where to find them!

Louise Simpson helps busy people to get more done and restore balance in their homes, tackling both the emotional and physical barriers. Happy to work virtually and in person.

www.LouiseSimpsonCoaching.co.uk

A Challenge Can Be an Opportunity

A Challenge Can Be an Opportunity

Metka Lebar

"When we least expect it, life sets us a challenge to test our courage and willingness to change." - Paulo Coelho

We live in unprecedented times where reality is abruptly changing in front of our eyes. How we respond is key.

The one mistake we tend to do when in panic is trying to push harder doing what we have always done. We'd better stop. Disrupt the automatic response. A challenge is a call to change and the first step to change is to stop doing what you have been doing and to stop being who you were up until this moment.

Assess what is really going on. Not everything becomes impossible in times of crisis. There are some things you can keep doing and there are others that you need to change.

Acceptance is the next important key. »This is how it is now,« is a mantra of strength. When you say yes to the unknown and embrace the outcome with an open mind, you can begin discovering your greater potential.

Think creatively to move beyond the challenge into opportunity. Search for alternatives to achieving your goals. You may even discover a better way of reaching them. A challenge is an opportunity to reassess what really matters and to strike a new path to higher peaks. You can do it!

Metka Lebar is a bestselling author, certified hypnotherapist, creativity, communication and spiritual life coach who helps people activate their true potential.
https://www.accessoneness.com/challenge-kit/

This Too Will Pass...

This Too Will Pass...

Paul Vandenberghe

"Everything will be all right in the end. If it's not all right, it is not yet the end."- Patel, Hotel Manager, The Best Exotic Marigold Hotel

Those who cannot remember the past are condemned to repeat it, they say. Whilst this may be true, we must remember that life comes in waves, so if we learn the lessons of our own past and those of our friends and families we will be more resilient than we know.

A colleague recently lost their job and berated themselves on social media for feeling negative. I shared some thoughts. You are not alone. This has happened before and may happen again and you will be o.k. I wrote. You are stronger than you think and if all you suffer is the occasional down day, well, you are doing better than most, I added. Then I shared my own experience.

I have worked through three recessions over thirty years and in each one, I have lost a job. Whilst at the time, it was stressful and yes, I had down days, I did what I could and trusted that with the support of those around me, it would be all right in the end.

Think back to what our parents and grandparents lived through and one quickly realises that all this has happened before and if they could survive it (as we know they did), you will too.

Paul Vandenberghe has worked in Financial Markets for over three decades. A life-long learner, he is fascinated by why people, organisations and markets behave in the way they do. He has been a mentor for the Prince's Trust helping young entrepreneurs get established and grow, a Trustee of a leading charity and a committee member for a community group.

Simple Steps To Move Forward

Simple Steps To Move Forward

Cheri Shapley

"Do something you're never done before so you can be someone you've never been before."

The act of doing something, of working on a problem, leads to ideas coming to mind on how to solve the issue at hand. We try the idea, we learn if this helped or not. The "act of trying" gives us a sense of accomplishment.

1) Write down all those jobs that are on your mind. Anything that you believe is unfinished needs to be captured. Removing these thoughts from your mind, allows you to focus on one task at a time. Simply take a piece of paper for each item. Keep going until your mind is clear. Then we will sort these into buckets or piles. Remember we can come back at any time and sort through and change the bucket/pile.

2) Review each item and identify what your action is, what you need to do to make progress towards completing the job or project. Perhaps, you need to book an appointment or pick something up as the next step.

3) After you have decided on all the actions you need to do, set up a system of reminders that you review regularly.

4) Focus on what you can do to move the top three items forward.

Cheri is a wife, mom and lover of animals and people. Life has not always been easy, but always look for the sunny side to bring light to the world. **www.cherishapley.com**

Write Now!

Write Now!

Helen Vandenberghe

"If the book is true, it will find an audience that is meant to read it."- Wally Lamb

I really believe every small business owner should consider writing a book. That's right, even you. If you're good at what you do, you have expertise to impart to your clients. A book with your name on it can open doors to opportunities you never imagined before.

And there's no better time than NOW to get started.

Creating a book that could be published in **a matter of months** can galvanise you into action and create a focal point for all your marketing efforts.

Writing your book can help you to:

- Build Credibility - be seen as an expert in your field

- Get on Podcasts, Radio & TV

- Grow your Email List & Audience

- Create a powerful launch

- Attract Joint Venture Partners & Affiliates

- Land New Clients & Opportunities

To get started, consider these questions

1. What do you want your book to do for your business? Pick ONE primary goal (e.g. grow your email list or get me PR) and keep this in mind whilst you write.

2. Who is your audience? Who is your book targeted at? If your aim is to get clients for your business, then target your 'ideal client'.

3. What is a small but important topic you could write about? Don't try to write 'War and Peace'. A short but powerful book is easier to write and more likely to be read!

4. How can you schedule planning and writing time into your day? Plan it, put it in your diary and get started NOW!

Helen Vandenberghe helps coaches and entrepreneurs become successful, published authors, in-demand speakers and high-end course creators. Download your FREE Business Book Planner at **www.writeyourbook.biz**

Hacks for Working at Home

Hacks for Working at Home

Deborah Durbin

Everyone loves the idea of working from home, but the reality is that you will either end up working much harder, or you will become the master of procrastination!

Having worked from home for the past 22 years, I've learned a few hacks that come in handy when you work from home...

Set Yourself 30 Minute Tasks:

Set a timer on your phone and once that time is up, reflect on what you have done in that time. Get up and get a coffee or have a walk around the house and then set yourself another 30 minutes.

Treat Your Work as You Would If You Were in The Workplace:

You wouldn't take a personal call from your partner in the middle of a meeting in the office. Make sure your friends and family know that you are working. If necessary, put a sign on your office door.

Take a Proper lunch Break:

It's all too easy to grab a snack from the kitchen and take it back to your desk and continue working. Close the office door and move to another room and make yourself a sandwich or some soup and switch off for a full hour.

Schedule Your Day:

Every evening, schedule the following day. I always clear my emails first thing in the morning and make any calls I need to make, giving me the rest of the day to get work done.

Get Outside:

If at all possible, take your office outside. The sounds of nature and the sun on your face will make you feel better. You'll feel so much better for it and will still be productive.

Deborah Durbin is an award-winning journalist, author of 14 books and a property developer. You can find out more about her at https:

https://deborahdurbin.wixsite.com/mysite

Take a Step Back

Take a Step Back

Joanna Edera

"The only thing that is constant is change." - Anonymous

When we encounter something that's unfamiliar, unpleasant, or challenging, we tend to panic and make rash decisions. Oftentimes, this leads us to follow how the majority responds to that situation - and this does not always end well.

When faced with a situation that's new to you, it's best to take a step back, to get a look from a different perspective, and then decide. When taking a step back, here are the things to think about.

1) What are you really worried about? Most of the time, the challenging situation is nothing to be alarmed about. We tend to worry when we see others worry. Don't allow yourself to fall into this trap.

2) Did your goal change because of what's happening? If not, proceed as planned. You might have to change a few steps and methods along the way to adapt, but aside from that, nothing has changed. So, carry on.

3) If your goal has been affected, think of ways to modify your goal. You don't have to completely change it. Small alterations are enough to get you up and running most of the time.

We know that change is inevitable, therefore, we should learn how to respond better to change and what better way than to take a step back before you take the next step.

Joanna Edera is a virtual assistant, project manager, and communications manager. She's passionate about productivity, learning, and adding value to the lives of others.

https://www.instagram.com/joannanoriel/

A Smile And A Thank-you.

A Smile And A Thank-you.

Barbara Ayers

'Smile at strangers and you just might change a life.'- Steve Maraboli

In these troubling times, when no one quite knows what to do, and we're figuring out the new rules of life and business, try to give a smile or a thank-you.

Give a smile to the stranger you pass in the street, the neighbour you only know to nod to. A friend you may meet. They all have worries or concerns and a smile from you can make the day a little less burdensome.

Saying 'Thank-you' for services done means a lot. People that are working tirelessly in our hospitals, shops, care homes & call centres. Delivery people, refuse collectors, road sweepers and countless others are all providing vital services, so we can run our businesses, and live life as normally as possible.

And for the homeless, remember that circumstances put them there. Fewer of us are carrying cash, so they too are suffering economically. You may want to give help financially, which is commendable, but if you can have a chat with them, it will be appreciated. It's a long day and night on the streets or staying in a hostel for the first time - with nothing to do, and no money in your pocket.

And when this horror ends and we start to get back to

normality, please a smile, or a chat, or a 'Thank-you', would maybe brighten someone's day. Remember that in some ways it has brought the best out of people. and let's keep that feeling going.

Barbara Ayers lives in North Somerset and has a lifetime experience of supporting others. As a mother and grandmother, aged 78, She has enjoyed working with children, In the preschool setting, Breakfast Clubs, After School clubs for 23 years.

Would You Love To Write Your Own Book?

Curating this book has been a wonderful, if somewhat hectic experience. We literally went from idea to manuscript in 21 days.

We were able to do this because all of the authors followed the blueprint and guidelines we provided and actually delivered their brilliant content on time, and in the style that works best for this sort of publication.

We've also had quite a bit of experience helping entrepreneurs, coaches and thought leaders to get their own books out into the world.

I'm more widely known as a business mentor, and for writing business articles and books like **'Get Clients Fast'** however, over the past five years I've been helping my VIP clients to get their books **written, published and sold.**

With my team, I help people with a big idea to **go from blank page to bestseller** in a matter of months rather than years.

We specialise in helping **non-fiction** authors to create a simple but powerful small book to help grow their business or champion their cause.

This is ideal for you if you want to:

- Create a short but powerful book to promote your business or cause
- Gain more prestige, become known as an expert and charge higher fees

- Share your knowledge and ideas with readers all over the world

- Take the fast path to becoming a published author

To discover how we can help you write, market & publish your first or next book in as little as 90 days visit:

www.WriteYourBook.Biz

Go on...Give a little

There are so many worthwhile charities helping to fight the recent health crisis from providing critical care to funding medical research.

We'd love it if you could join us in donating to these amazing organisations.

For those in the UK, we've chosen the NHS Charities Together campaign.

Donate to NHS Charities Together at: https://bit.ly/2L6xURw

For our international readers, we've chosen The World Health Organisation (WHO) which is leading and coordinating the global effort, supporting countries to prevent, detect, and respond to the pandemic.

Donate to the World Health Organisation at: https://bit.ly/2WcJAJ5

We're in this together.

Thank you.

Acknowledgements

I would like to share my thanks and appreciation to so many people for their help in creating this book.

Firstly, my Mum - Barbara Ayers - for her unending encouragement, along with her brilliant and very patient proofreading. Deborah Durbin for her inspiration and support, Matt Ayers for 'middle of the night' emergency tech help! Further read throughs and endless enthusiasm by Paul Vandenberghe and Jan Edmiston helped enormously.

Joanna Edera for her extremely quick and helpful administrative support whilst in 'lockdown' in The Philippines. For Julie Brown for her kind offer to provide PR support to the project. And finally, our wonderful writers who co-created this book just for you.

Alison Haitana

Alison Thomson

Amanda Fitzgerald

Amanda O'Rourke

Andree Funnell

Anna-Maria Hawke

Annie P. Ruggles

Azmina Ahamed

Barbara Ayers

Barbara Ellison

Carol Davies

Carol May

Caroline Esterson

Cheri Shapley

Cherry-Ann Carew

Claire Carroll

Danielle Haley

Debs de Vries

Deborah Durbin

Dorothy Martin-Neville

Dr Kevin Lentin

Dr. Trina Boice

Genny Sapiro

Irene Gannaway

Irina Strunina

Janey Lee Grace

Jenn Summers

Joanna Edera

Jo Cowlin

Jo Soley

Julie Brown

Kerrie Maitland

LaFaye Pye

Louise Simpson

Lynette Allen

Marianne Dupuis Janin

Marla Hall

Mary Silver MSW

Melesha Bailey

Metka Lebar

Minesh Baxi

Minling Chuang

Naomi Martell-Bundock

Paul Vandenberghe

Rachel Smets

Regina Bergman

Rosemary Cunningham

Sandra Noble

Sarah Brunel-while

Shalini Menezes

Teresa Blount

Tom Matzen

Valerie Dwyer

Vatsala Shukla

Wendy Gannaway

Zoe Goode

Are You Ready To Rise?

www.readytorise.co.uk

Printed in Great Britain
by Amazon